HUSTLE WITH PURPOSE

Hustle With Purpose

Darien M Adair

Contents

Dedication vi

CHAPTER ONE - The Real Face of Adaptability 1

CHAPTER TWO - Embrace the Grind, But Work Smart 8

CHAPTER THREE - Failure is Fuel 14

CHAPTER FOUR - The Art of the Pivot 20

CHAPTER FIVE - The Strength in Support Sys-tems 26

CHAPTER SIX - Mental Strength and Re-silience 32

CHAPTER SEVEN - Balancing Ambition and Well-Being 38

CHAPTER EIGHT - The power of focus 45

CHAPTER NINE - Scaling Your Success 52

CHAPTER TEN - Leaving a legacy 59

IV |

About the Author 66

Closing Statement 68

Index 69

© 2024 Darien Adair - Hustle with Purpose

All rights reserved. No part of this publication may be reproduced, distributed, or transmitted in any form or by any means, including photocopying, recording, or other electronic or mechanical methods, without the prior written permission of the author, except in the case of brief quotations embodied in critical reviews and certain other noncommercial uses permitted by copyright law.

Disclaimer: This book is intended to provide helpful and practical advice on the topics discussed. It is not a substitute for professional advice, and readers should consult qualified professionals for specific guidance in areas such as financial planning, mental health, or career advice. The author and publisher are not responsible for any outcomes related to the application of the ideas presented in this book.
ISBN: [9798348141707]
Published by Darien Adair
Indianapolis, Indiana

First Edition: December 2024

Thank you

Dedication to my beloved wife, who has been my unwavering support throughout this journey.

To my dear Mother, the nurturer of a problem solver.

To my brothers, bound by blood and choice, exemplifying true brotherhood.
Your unwavering faith in me has made all the difference.

And to all the dreamers who dare to aspire to greatness – Keep believing, keep striving, keep evolving.

This book is a tribute to each and every one of you.

Acknowledgements

First and foremost, I give all praise to God.

To my mother, thank you for every sacrifice and lesson.
To my siblings: Danita, Shapore, Geri, Rianna, Ebony, Charon, and Mikey (Damone) – thank you for shaping who I am.

To my closest friends who became brothers: AD (Alan-drius Allen), Alex Harris, Dominique Fox, JB (James Bur-rell), Halston Thomas, LP (Larry Bowen), CreShawn Burruss, Steven Thomas, Dewayne Humphrey, AJ Brown Sr, Austin Johnson, Jordan Dehart, Drew Bernard, Antwan Robinson, and Bryon Mills – thank you for your unwavering support.

To my cousins: Tomisha Barker, Marcus Adair, Sean Adair Jr, and George Logan – I appreciate you and the support.

For guidance and wisdom: My uncles Ricky (Sean Adair Sr) and Anthony Tucker, my step-dad William, father-in-law Fred, and mentor Grady McGee.

To everyone who supported this journey – thank you.

With gratitude,
Darien

One

The Real Face of Adaptability

Life in Indianapolis – Naptown as we locals call it – taught me early that adaptability isn't just about changing with the times; it's about creating your own path when the usual routes don't feel right. Growing up here, I saw too many people trying to fit into boxes others built for them. Whether it was career choices, lifestyle decisions, or creative pursuits, there was always this pressure to follow the "proven" path.

But here's what I learned: the most powerful form of adaptation isn't about fitting into someone else's mold – it's about breaking it and building your own. I started noticing this pattern in everything I did. When others zigged, something in me naturally wanted to zag. Not just to be different, but because I knew there had to be more than one way to reach a destination.

Learning from the Family Tree

Being the youngest of eight children was my first masterclass in adaptation. Each of my siblings brought their own flavor to my life, teaching me different ways to navigate the world. My sisters – Danita, Shapore, Geri, and Rianna – showed me the power of resilience and creativity. They were my first examples of how to make something out of nothing, turning everyday situations into opportunities for growth.

My sisters' influence didn't stop there. Ebony, the last of my five sisters, brought her own unique energy to my life. Then there were my brothers – Charon and Damone (we called him Mikey). Each one shaped different aspects of who I would become. Charon showed me how to stand firm in my beliefs. And Mikey... Mikey was special. He wasn't just my brother; he was my blueprint for authenticity.

The Impact of Brotherhood

Mikey, known to his friends as "Black" or "Country Black," had this way of moving through life that was completely his own. He didn't just tell me to be myself; he showed me how. "Aye lil bro," he'd say, particularly when talking about my music, "Ain't nobody colder than you with that music sh**....don't ever stop." His words weren't just encouragement – they were permission to be unapologetically myself.

When we lost Mikey in 2008, it shook our whole world. But even in loss, there were lessons about adaptability and growth. It taught me that life's greatest challenges don't just test us; they transform us. Through that difficult time, I discovered another kind of family – friends who stepped up to become brothers.

The Extended Family

AD and Alex became my closest brothers, my voice of reason. They were there to help me stay calm when my thoughts drifted toward reckless decisions, even opening their homes to me when I needed a place of peace. AD's house was like my second home during those times.

Some bonds were inherited through Mikey, like JB (James Burrell) and Halston. They were his closest friends who, over years of proving their genuine care for my wellbeing, earned their place as my brothers too. Then there's LP (Larry Bowen), our cousin who became everyone's favorite family member, turning his house into our sanctuary of laughter and good times.

Dominique Fox became the brother who prioritized my mental health above all else, while CreShawn Burruss stood as my longest-standing friend – over 20 years of brotherhood and being solid that started in childhood and never wavered. Stevie and DeWayne entered the circle and quickly became irreplaceable parts of our brotherhood, each adding their own strength to our extended family. These relationships, along with brothers like AJ Brown Sr, Austin Johnson, and others, showed me that family isn't just about blood – it's about who stands with you through life's adaptations.

Building Your Adaptability Toolkit: Practical Exercises

The Daily Pivot Challenge
Start your day by choosing one habit or routine to switch up. How does this small change shift your mindset? Take some time to reflect on your feelings about this change and what it reveals about you.

The Resourcefulness Workout
Pick a mundane task you do regularly, and brainstorm three different ways to tackle it. Experiment with each method over the course of a week and see if any of these new approaches work better than your usual one.

3. The Comfort Zone Stretcher
Each month, challenge yourself to do something that pushes you out of your comfort zone, even just a little. Keep a journal to track your experiences, and don't forget to celebrate the small wins and the lessons you learn along the way.

4. The Problem-Solving Sprint
When you hit a roadblock, set a timer for 10 minutes and jot down as many potential solutions as you can, no matter

how far-fetched they might seem. Use this exercise to uncover hidden opportunities within your challenges.

Implementation Tips:
Remember, it's all about progress, not perfection. Start small and stay consistent as you build your adaptability skills.

Key Adaptability Principles:

- Embrace Discomfort: View challenges as teachers rather than enemies.
- Stay Flexible in Method, Firm in Purpose: While your end goals may remain the same, your methods might need to adapt.
- Build Your Support System: Don't hesitate to lean on others; true adaptability involves community.
- Keep Your Core Values: Being adaptable doesn't mean losing your identity; it's about expressing yourself in new ways.

Reflection Questions:

- What aspects of your life could use a bit more adaptability?
- Who in your life supports you during times of change?
- What can you do today to strengthen your adaptability skills?

"Remember, adaptability is not about reaching a final destination; it's a lifelong journey filled with growth, learning, and transformation. Each challenge you face is a chance to enhance this valuable life skill."

Being adaptable will create opportunities to many doors. Your purpose will lead you through the right doors.

Two

Embrace the Grind, But Work Smart

Sometimes the most profound wisdom comes from unexpected places. I remember standing at a gas station, listening to a clerk vent about his job frustrations. As I started to offer encouragement about it being part of the process, a stranger behind me spoke up with words that would stick with me forever: "A job stands for Just Over Broke." When I asked him to elaborate, his response hit even harder: "Companies pay you to forget your own dreams so you can help build theirs. I'll gladly pay you to work over 40 hours so that I don't have to, and I'll focus on other ways to profit

That conversation became a turning point in how I viewed work and productivity. In that moment I understood "TIME IS MONEY SO DON'T WASTE IT. " It wasn't about working less – it was about working with a purpose, about being intentional with every hour invested.

The Busy Trap

My time as both a manufacturing manager and a store manager taught me this lesson the hard way. I fell into the common trap of thinking that doing everything myself was the only way to ensure things were done right. I'd pour 110% into each day, running from task to task, putting out fires, and micro-managing every detail. At day's end, I'd be exhausted, but when I looked at what I'd actually accomplished – what needle I'd actually moved – the results were sobering.

Being busy isn't the same as being productive. I was like a hamster on a wheel, expending enormous energy but not really getting anywhere. Each day was a blur of activity, but the bigger goals, the real priorities, weren't being met. Something had to change.

The Smart Pivot

The transformation began when I started focusing not just on solutions, but on potential roadblocks. Instead of rushing head first into tasks, I began mapping out possible issues that might arise along the way. More importantly, I learned to leverage both people and resources effectively.

I discovered that delegation isn't about passing off work – it's about recognizing and utilizing strengths. Some team members excelled at organization, others at customer service, and still others at problem-solving. By matching tasks to talents, everything ran more smoothly, and results improved dramatically. It also gave me more room to learn more and perfect my skillsets.

The Power of Multiple Skillsets

My approach to learning multiple skills came from an unusual place: fear. While many of my friends had clear career paths, I worried about putting all my eggs in one basket. This fear drove me to develop a range of abilitie drawing, music, coding, acting – as backup plans. But something unexpected happened along the way: learnir became therapeutic. Each new skill not only provided another potential path but also enriched my understand of the others.

Knowledge truly is power, but it's not just about accumulating information. It's about understanding how different skills and perspectives can work together. Each new ability I developed gave me another tool for problem-solving, another way to approach challenges.

Smart Work Principles

- Plan Before You Execute
  - Map out potential obstacles before starting
  - Identify key resources and skills needed
  - Set clear, measurable objectives
- Leverage Team Strengths
  - Recognize that you can't (and shouldn't) do everything
  - Match tasks to individual talents

- Build systems that scale beyond your personal capacity

Continuous Learning
- Develop multiple skills as backup plans
- Let each new ability inform and enhance others
- Stay curious and adaptable

Focus on Impact
- Regularly assess if activities move the needle
- Eliminate or delegate tasks that don't serve the bigger picture
- Measure progress against clear goals

Practical Application: The Smart Work Audit

- Take a week to track your activities and evaluate them using these criteria:
- Does this task require my specific skills?
- Could someone else do this better?
- Is this moving me toward my larger goals?
- What potential obstacles might I encounter?
- How can I leverage resources or team members more effectively?

Key Takeaway

Working smart isn't about cutting corners or finding shortcuts. It's about being intentional with your energy, leveraging available resources effectively, and staying focused on what truly matters. Sometimes the hardest worker isn't the one who does everything, but the one who knows how to orchestrate the right pieces at the right time.

- Reflection Questions
- What tasks in your current routine could benefit from smarter execution?
- Are you building skills that complement each other?
- How can you better leverage the strengths of those around you?

"Remember: Your energy is your most precious resource. Invest it wisely, and don't let being busy become a substitute for being effective."

The grind isn't about wearing yourself down - it's about discovering your true potential, even if you have to fail to find it.

Three

Failure is Fuel

Life's greatest lessons often come from our darkest moments. For me, that moment came when I found myself in trouble with the law. It was a turning point that taught me something profound: sometimes you have to lose everything to find what truly matters.

Finding Strength in Solitude
Behind those walls, I faced a reality where I had no choice but to look inward. The system was simple: work or face solitary confinement and potentially lose good time off your sentence. While this might seem like forced motivation, it taught me an invaluable lesson about routine and discipline. Every day, following the same schedule, I began to understand that structure wasn't just about compliance – it was about building a foundation for growth.
In that solitude, when all external supports were stripped away, I discovered that God was all I needed. This wasn't just a spiritual awakening; it was a fundamental shift in how

I approached challenges. When everything else was gone, faith remained, teaching me that true strength comes from something deeper than circumstance.

The Foundation of Success

Throughout my journey, I've learned that success isn't just about human effort. Every time I relied solely on my own abilities or put my faith entirely in others, I fell short. But when I put God first, doors opened in unexpected ways. This isn't just about religion – it's about understanding that there's something greater than ourselves at work in our journey to success.

Learning Through Business Failures

My journey to success, while building a brand came with its own set of hard lessons. Initially, I made the classic entrepreneur's mistake – targeting friends and family as my primary market. While it seemed logical to start with my inner circle, I quickly learned that this approach had a fatal flaw. Friends and family often expect discounts and freebies, and when you're starting out, your profit margins can't support that kind of generosity.

This failure led to an innovative pivot. After seeing a Popeyes commercial and discovering the disconnect between the brand's public face and its ownership, I had an epiphany. I approached my close friend and brother, Drew Bernard, with an unconventional proposition: he would be the face of the brand while I operated as the owner behind the scenes. This strategic move wasn't about deception – it was about creating a buffer that allowed the business to grow sustainably.

The Power of Proactive Thinking

One of my costliest lessons came from reactive production. I'd pour my heart into creating clothing items without validating the market, leading to unsold inventory and wasted resources. The shift to pre-orders and drop-shipping wasn't just about changing business models – it was about transforming failure into a smarter approach. This allowed me to focus on my art while eliminating unnecessary risks.

Turning Failure Into Strategy

Embrace the Reset

- Every failure is an opportunity to rebuild with better foundation
- Use setbacks to reassess your approach and priorities
- Let each mistake guide you toward more strategic thinking

Build Sustainable Systems

- Create routines that support your goals
- Focus on processes rather than just outcomes

- Learn to distinguish between what you can and cannot control

Adapt Your Approach

- Be willing to pivot when traditional methods aren't working
- Think creatively about solutions to common problems
- Use setbacks as market research

Stay Grounded in Faith

- Remember that success comes from something greater than ourselves
- Use spiritual strength as a foundation for business decisions
- Let your values guide your choices

Practical Application: The Failure Analysis Framework

When you encounter a setback, ask yourself:

- What assumptions led to this failure?
- What systems or habits need to change?
- How can this experience improve my next attempt?
- What strengths did this challenge reveal?

Key Takeaway

"Failure isn't the opposite of success – it's a crucial part of the journey. Every setback carries the seeds of future triumph if you have the wisdom to learn from it and the courage to keep moving forward."

Reflection Questions

- What recent failure could be redirecting you to a better path?
- How can you build more sustainable systems in your life and work?
- Are you learning from your setbacks, or just experiencing them?

"Remember: The size of your success is often determined by how well you use your failures as fuel for growth."

Look at failure as redirection, not a dead end. Your purpose isn't lost in the detour; sometimes it's found there.

Four

The Art of the Pivot

Sometimes the bravest thing you can do is change direction. In business, relationships, and life, knowing when and how to pivot isn't just a skill – it's an art form that can mean the difference between stagnation and growth.

Learning Through Design

My journey in brand development taught me this lesson repeatedly. Each time I made a mistake or halted production because something was no longer trending, it wasn't just about making changes – it was about learning the craft more. These weren't failures; they were necessary redirections that forced me to understand my industry better.

Every pivot in design taught me something new. Being out of season with certain pieces wasn't just a setback – it was a lesson learned. Every time I thought I was ready, there was more to learn. Sometimes I would switch directions on a idea in the moment. These moments of redirection became opportunities for deeper learning and growth.

The Spiritual Compass

The most significant pivot in my life came when I decided to truly put God first in everything. This wasn't just about adding prayer to my routine – it was about fundamentally changing how I approached decisions. I began dedicating 30 minutes to an hour each day in prayer about the direction of my life and career. As the Bible tells us in James 2:17, "Faith without works is dead," so I knew that while prayer was essential, I also needed to actively work toward what I believed I could achieve.

This spiritual pivot changed everything, but I was careful to maintain authenticity in my relationship with God. I never wanted these conversations to feel transactional – it wasn't about asking for success; it was about seeking guidance and wisdom. God became my compass, helping me navigate decisions big and small.

The Peace Priority

One of the most crucial lessons I've learned about pivoting is that your peace should always trump what stresses you. Whether it's relationships that weigh you down, self-doubt that holds you back, or jobs that drain your energy, sometimes you have to pivot away from what's comfortable but not serving your growth.

This applies across all areas of life:

1. In relationships: Sometimes you need to distance yourself from connections that don't align with your growth
2. In career: A steady paycheck isn't worth the cost of constant stress and no fulfillment
3. In personal growth: Old habits and mindsets might be familiar, but they might also be holding you back

Knowing When to Pivot

My process for determining when to pivot starts with prayer – asking God for clear signs about whether to step away from situations that aren't bringing peace. But beyond spiritual guidance, there are practical indicators that help signal when it's time for change:

The Peace Test

- Are you consistently stressed or at peace?
- Does this situation align with your values?
- Is your current path sustainable for your wellbeing?

The Growth Assessment
- Are you learning and developing?
- Does this direction align with your long-term vision?
- Are you seeing progress, even if it's slow?

The Alignment Check

- Does this path align with your purpose?
- Are your actions matching your beliefs?
- Is this taking you closer to or further from your goals?

Practical Steps for Pivoting
Seek Guidance

- Start with prayer and reflection
- Consult trusted mentors
- Research your new direction thoroughly

Plan Your Transition

- Set clear objectives for the pivot
- Create a timeline for change
- Identify potential obstacles and solutions

Execute with Purpose

- Move decisively once you've made your decision
- Keep your end goal in focus
- Stay flexible as you adapt to your new direction

Key Takeaway

Pivoting isn't about abandoning ship – it's about steering toward better waters. Whether in business, relationships, or personal growth, the ability to recognize and execute strategic changes while staying true to your core values is essential for long-term success.

Reflection Questions

1. What areas of your life might need a strategic pivot?
2. Are you holding onto anything that's compromising your peace?
3. How can you better align your daily actions with your long-term vision?

"**Remember: Every pivot is an opportunity for growth, and every redirection can lead to better alignment with your purpose – as long as you're moving with intention and staying true to your values.**"

Life will force you to pivot, but purpose will show you who you need to pivot with. No great vision stands alone.

Five

The Strength in Support Systems

Until I was 25 years old, I thought success was a solo journey. It wasn't that support wasn't available – I just never asked for it. I had convinced myself that no one wanted to help, but the reality was, I had never given them the chance. This mindset shift taught me one of life's most valuable lessons: strength isn't about doing it all alone; it's about knowing when and how to lean on others.

The Power of Asking
The moment I started asking for help, I discovered something profound: there were countless helping hands ready to lift me up. Not necessarily with money, but with something far more valuable – their time, their ideas, their support. What I once saw as weakness – needing help – turned out to be one of my greatest strengths.

Layers of Support

Like a well-built house, a strong support system needs different elements working together. Each person in my support network brings something unique and invaluable to the table.

Spiritual Foundation First and foremost, I turn to God for all guidance. This spiritual foundation ensures that every decision, whether personal or professional, aligns with my core values and purpose.

Family Pillars My family's unwavering belief in me has been a constant source of strength. Their simple question, "Is there anything you can't do?" wasn't just encouragement – it was a reminder of their faith in my abilities. My step-dad William and father-in-law Fred have become go-to sources for personal advice, while my uncles Ricky (Sean Adair Sr) and Anthony Tucker offer wisdom that only comes from years of life experience.

The Heart of Support My wife has been "Team Darien" from the beginning, not just supporting my dreams but actively pushing me toward greatness. She's my safe space when frustration hits, my soundboard when ideas need refining, and my emotional anchor through all of life's ups and downs.

Extended Family Strength Cousins like Tomisha Barker, Marcus Adair, Sean Adair Jr, and George Logan have each played crucial roles in my journey. Their support shows that family bonds can be one of your greatest assets when pursuing your dreams.

Professional Guidance For business wisdom, I turn to mentors like Grady McGee. His "This will make a man out of you" and "You have to constantly move the needle" weren't just words – they were investments in my future. He saw potential in me and helped shape my path to success.

Organized Support Sometimes support comes from unexpected places. My wife's friend/sister Brittany brought an organized mindset to the table, breaking down overwhelming goals into manageable tasks. Her belief that my success meant collective success showed me how true support systems think beyond individual achievement.

Building Your Support Network
Start with Humility

- Recognize that asking for help is a strength, not a weakness
- Be open about your needs and goals
- Acknowledge your limitations

Diversify Your Support

- Seek different perspectives and expertise
- Build relationships across various areas of life

- Understand that different people can support you in different ways

Nurture Relationships

- Be willing to give as much as you receive
- Show gratitude consistently
- Celebrate others' successes as they celebrate yours

Maintain Boundaries

- Respect people's time and energy
- Be clear about expectations
- Know when to step back and when to lean in

The Reciprocity Principle

- A strong support system isn't just about receiving – it's about giving back. For everyone mentioned in this book, I would give the shirt off my back, and I know they'd do the same. This mutual commitment creates a network that's both resilient and sustainable.

Practical Application: Support System Audit

- Take time to assess your support network:

- Who do you turn to for different types of advice?
- Are there gaps in your support system?
- How can you better show up for those who support you?
- What skills or resources can you offer to others?

Key Takeaway

Success is never truly a solo achievement. Behind every accomplishment is a network of support, guidance, and encouragement. The sooner you embrace this truth and actively build your support system, the stronger your foundation for success becomes.

Reflection Questions

- Are you fully utilizing the support available to you?
- How can you better reciprocate the support you receive?
- What areas of your life need additional support?

"Remember: Strength isn't found in isolation – it's built through connection, trust, and mutual support."

They say it takes a village, but it takes a leader's vision to guide the way. Let your circle fuel your fire, then let your fire light their path.

Six

Mental Strength and Resilience

Mental strength isn't just about powering through challenges – it's about building daily habits that reinforce your resilience and help you maintain clarity when facing life's obstacles.

The Power of Daily Reinforcement
One of the most effective tools I've found is using technology to maintain a positive mindset. I download apps that deliver daily motivational messages to my phone. These aren't just random quotes – they're daily reminders to stay focused and motivated. But the real power comes from taking these messages a step further: standing in front of the mirror and speaking words of encouragement to myself. This isn't about ego; it's about programming your mind for success.

Long walks have become another crucial part of my mental strength routine. These aren't just about exercise – they're opportunities for clear thinking, problem-solving, and mental reset. Sometimes the best solutions come when you're simply giving your mind space to breathe and process.

Learning from the Master of Patience

My mother taught me one of the most valuable lessons about mental strength through her example. Raising eight children, each with distinctly different personalities, requires a level of patience that most people can't imagine. Where others might have crumbled under the pressure, she maintained her composure and managed to give each of us what we needed.

Watching her juggle the demands of such a large family taught me how to handle multiple challenges simultaneously. It wasn't just about getting things done – it was about maintaining your peace while doing it. This lesson has proven invaluable in both personal and professional situations, showing me that mental strength often manifests as calm in the midst of chaos.

Navigating Self-Doubt

The challenge of having multiple talents can sometimes feel like a burden. I've faced numerous moments of doubt, questioning which path to pursue when you're capable in many areas. Should I focus on art? Music? Business? Each

talent pulled me in a different direction, and the fear of choosing wrong could be a waste of time.
Even in my clothing brand, after spending hours on production, self-doubt would creep in about releasing certain pieces. These moments taught me that doubt isn't always a warning sign – sometimes it's just part of the creative process. The key is not letting it stop you from taking action.

Building Mental Resilience

The cornerstone of maintaining mental strength is learning to stay calm under pressure.

When challenges arise, I've learned to: Take a Pause

- Give yourself permission to step back
- Create space for clear thinking
- Use breathing as an anchor

Shift Perspective

- Look at situations from different angles
- Consider alternative solutions
- Find opportunities in challenges

Maintain Daily Practices

- Use technology for positive reinforcement

Practice self-affirmation
Make time for mental clarity walks

Learn from Experience

- Document what works for you
- Build on successful strategies
- Adjust approaches as needed

Practical Mental Strength Exercises 1. The Mirror Motivation

- Start each morning with positive self-talk
- Speak your goals out loud
- Acknowledge your progress and potential

2. The Clarity Walk

- Schedule regular walks for thinking
- Leave your phone on silent
- Focus on one challenge or goal during each walk

3. The Pause Practice

- When stressed, take three deep breaths
- Ask yourself: "How else can I look at this?"
- Consider what you can learn from the situation

4. The Gratitude Reset

- List three things going well
- Acknowledge your current strengths
- Remember past challenges you've overcome

Key Takeaway

Mental strength isn't about never feeling doubt or stress – it's about having systems in place to manage these feelings effectively. It's about building daily habits that reinforce your resilience and help you maintain perspective when facing challenges.

Reflection Questions

- What daily practices could you implement to strengthen your mental resilience?
- How do you currently handle moments of self-doubt?
- What lessons about mental strength have you learned from others in your life?

"Remember: True mental strength isn't about being tough all the time – it's about knowing how to regain your balance when life throws you off center."

Look at mental strength as your engine, balance as your wheels, and well-being as your fuel. One powers you forward, one keeps you on course, and one keeps you running.

Seven

Balancing Ambition and Well-Being

Sometimes the biggest obstacles to success aren't external challenges – they're our own habits and mindsets. I learned this lesson the hard way, burning the candle at both ends, staying up all hours of the night trying to solve problems, and working overtime more than necessary. It took falling asleep during regular working hours and in mid-conversation with people to realize something had to change.

The Wake-Up Call

Ambition is powerful, but without balance, it can become destructive. When you're finding yourself nodding off during important conversations or struggling to stay present during regular business hours, that's not dedication – that's depletion. Your body and mind will eventually force you to rest, either on your terms or theirs.

Creating Sustainable Rhythms

The solution isn't working less – it's working smarter. Here's how I restructured my approach:

Prioritize Rest

- Commit to getting as close to 8 hours of sleep as possible
- Recognize that rest isn't lazy – it's essential
- Understand that fatigue compromises everything else

Time Blocking

- Allocate 1-2 hours for each task or hobby
- Stick to hard cutoff times
- Respect the boundaries you set

Fresh Perspectives

- Use breaks between sessions to gain new viewpoints
- Allow ideas to marinate
- Return to projects with renewed creativity

Redefining Success

Success isn't just about reaching the end goal – it's about the journey and what you learn along the way. I've come to define success as being at least 1% better than the day before. This shift in perspective changes everything:

- Small improvements compound over time
- Every step of the journey has value
- There are no shortcuts to meaningful achievement

You can't cut corners on the path to success. Every challenge, every setback, every lesson shapes who you become and makes the achievement more meaningful.

The Art of Separation

One of the most powerful principles I've learned is the importance of boundaries. Just as many workplaces say "leave your problems at the door," I've learned to "keep your personal life private and leave your work life at work."

This clear separation creates space for:

- Better focus in each area
- Deeper presence in the moment
- Reduced stress and mental clutter
- More effective problem-solving

Practical Balance Strategies 1. The Sleep Reset

- Make sleep a non-negotiable priority
- Create a consistent bedtime routine
- Honor your body's need for rest

2. The Time Block Method

- Schedule specific times for each activity
- Set clear start and end times
- Respect the boundaries you create

3. The Transition Ritual

- Develop routines for switching between work and personal mode
- Create clear markers for ending work time
- Establish practices for beginning personal time

4. The Progress Check

- Review your 1% improvements regularly
- Celebrate small wins
- Adjust strategies as needed

Balance in Action

Balance isn't about perfect equilibrium – it's about intentional allocation of your energy. Consider:

Energy Management

- Identify your peak performance hours

- Schedule demanding tasks during high-energy times
- Reserve lower-energy periods for routine tasks

Boundary Setting

- Communicate your limits clearly
- Stick to your cutoff times
- Learn to say no when necessary

Recovery Planning

- Build in regular breaks
- Plan for both daily and weekly recovery
- Make time for activities that rejuvenate you

Key Takeaway

Balance isn't about doing less – it's about doing things more effectively. When you honor the boundaries between different areas of your life and prioritize sustainable practices, you actually accomplish more in the long run.

Reflection Questions

1. Where in your life do you need clearer boundaries?
2. What would being 1% better look like for you today?
3. How can you create more sustainable patterns in your daily routine?

"Remember: True achievement isn't about sacrificing everything for success – it's about creating a sustainable approach that allows you to maintain your drive while protecting your well-being."

Keep your balance but don't forget to stay focus.

Eight

The power of focus

In a world full of distractions, the ability to focus has become a superpower. But focus isnt just about willpower – its about creating systems that support your concentration and protect your attention.

Managing Digital Distractions

One of the most effective changes I've made is taking control of my screen time. It's not enough to just say you'll use your phone less – you need concrete boundaries. I use my phone's screen time notifications and set specific caps on usage. More importantly, I've learned that sometimes the best way to handle distractions is to make them physically inaccessible – locking them in another room or leaving them in the car.

This isn't about depriving yourself of technology; it's about being intentional with your attention. When something truly matters, it deserves your undivided focus.

Strategic Prioritization

To maintain focus on what truly matters, I use the Eisenhower Matrix – a simple but powerful tool that hel[ps] categorize tasks based on their urgency and importance. Within each quadrant, I number tasks from greatest to le[ast] priority. This isn't just about organizing; it's about ensuri[ng] your energy goes to the right things at the right time. The matrix helps break down priorities into four categories:

1. Urgent and Important: Do immediately
2. Important but Not Urgent: Schedule for later
3. Urgent but Not Important: Delegate if possible
4. Neither Urgent nor Important: Eliminate

This system doesn't just track tasks – it tracks progress. Each completed item becomes a visible marker of movement toward your goals.

Time Blocking for Multiple Interests

Having multiple passions can be both a blessing and a challenge. The key is not trying to do everything at once, but rather giving each interest its dedicated time to shine. I allocate 30 minutes to 2 hours for each hobby or goal, creating focused blocks where that activity gets my complete attention.

When ideas for one project pop up while working on another – which happens often – I quickly jot them down for later. This simple practice keeps the creative flow going while maintaining current focus. It's about honoring both your present task and your future inspirations.

Creating Focus-Friendly Environments

Environment shapes focus. I've learned to surround myself only with tools relevant to the current task. When it's time for art, I create an artist's space – drawing pads, art books, brushes, and paint. Nothing else exists in that moment except what serves the creative process.

The only exception I would make is music, which actually enhances rather than disrupts my creativity. This isn't about rigid rules; it's about knowing what helps and what hinders your particular focus.

Practical Focus Strategies Digital Boundaries

- Set specific screen time limits
- Use app blockers during focus periods
- Create physical distance from distractions

Priority Management

- Use the Eisenhower Matrix for task organization
- Number tasks by importance within each category
- Track progress visually

Time Blocking

- Allocate specific time slots for each activity
- Use timers to maintain boundaries
- Keep a quick-capture tool for random ideas

Environment Design

- Create task-specific workspaces
- Remove irrelevant items
- Include only tools needed for current focus

Getting Back on Track

Even with the best systems, distractions happen. The key is having mechanisms to pull yourself back:

- Set timers as focus anchors
- Use environmental cues to maintain task awareness
- Keep your prioritized task list visible

Key Focus Principles

Elimination Before Optimization

- Remove distractions first
- Create barriers to interruption
- Simplify your environment

Structured Flexibility

- Use systems but allow for creative flow
- Honor both focus and inspiration

- Adapt methods to your working style

Progressive Improvement

- Start with manageable focus periods
- Build duration gradually
- Celebrate small wins

Implementation Tips
Start Small

- Begin with 30-minute focus blocks
- Gradually increase duration
- Build confidence through consistency

Track and Adjust
- Monitor what works for you
- Adjust systems as needed
- Keep what serves your focus

Plan for Interruptions
- Have a capture system ready
- Know how to get back on track
- Accept that some disruptions are inevitable

Key Takeaway

Focus isn't about perfect concentration – it's about creating environments and systems that support your attention. When you design your space and time intentionally, maintaining focus becomes more natural and sustainable.

Reflection Questions

1. What are your biggest focus disruptors?
2. How can you better design your environment for focus?
3. What systems could help you maintain attention on priority tasks?

"Remember: Focus is a skill that can be developed and strengthened through intentional practice and smart systems."

Focusing can turn plans into a legacy.

Nine

Scaling Your Success

Growth without wisdom is just expansion. True scaling requires learning when to let go, when to hold firm, and most importantly, when to listen to others.

The Control Paradox

One of my hardest but most valuable lessons came from trying to control everything. I thought being hands-on with every detail meant ensuring quality, but it actually meant limiting our potential. This hit home when I stubbornly pushed forward with a design despite a friend's suggestions for improvements. After production, customers made the exact same suggestions my friend had made earlier. This moment humbled me and opened my heart to a crucial truth: sometimes the best leadership means stepping back and listening.

The key isn't surrendering all control – it's being selective about where you maintain it. I learned to divide projects into categories from the start, keeping only what I'm best at and delegating the rest. What's fascinating is how this builds mutual trust. When you include people in your vision and give them real responsibility, they naturally want to excel. They're not just executing tasks; they're investing in shared success.

The Science of Scaling

Scaling isn't just about growing bigger – it's about growing smarter. I've developed comprehensive checklists that evolve with each project, ensuring quality control from the beginning. As we expand, so do these checkpoints, creating a dynamic system that grows with us.

One of the trickiest aspects of scaling is finding the right pace. Scale too quickly, and you risk audience fatigue – people get tired of seeing you everywhere. Scale too slowly, and you lose momentum – people get impatient waiting for what's next. The sweet spot lies in finding that perfect balance and maintaining it.

Aligning Vision with Action

Perhaps the greatest challenge in scaling is keeping everyone aligned with your vision, especially when you can't prove future outcomes. This is where track record becomes crucial – people need to have witnessed your capabilities to believe in your future directions. The key is including your team in the wins, making them stakeholders in the vision rather than just executors of tasks.

Clear communication becomes your most valuable tool:

- Regular updates on project direction
- Transparent sharing of status and progress
- Clear definition of roles and responsibilities

When everyone understands their part in the bigger picture, confusion decreases and collaboration increases.

Practical Scaling Strategies Smart Delegation

- Categorize project components early
- Match tasks to team strengths
- Maintain oversight without micromanaging

Quality Control

- Develop comprehensive checklists
- Update quality measures as you grow
- Build in feedback loops

Communication Systems

- Regular team updates
- Clear role definitions
- Open feedback channels

Growth Management

- Monitor market response
- Adjust pace based on feedback
- Balance exposure with demand

The Financial Foundation

One of the most crucial lessons in scaling is understanding the relationship between profit and growth. When you're profiting, the instinct might be to expand immediately. However, I've learned that it's often better to consolidate as much as possible first. Build your financial foundation until expansion becomes a necessity rather than just an option.

This approach:

- Builds financial security
- Creates scalable systems
- Allows for strategic rather than reactive growth

Core Principles for Scaling
Maintain Consistency

- Keep up with industry trends
- Deliver reliable quality
- Stay true to your mission

Value Alignment

- Let your core values guide growth
- Make decisions that align with your mission
- Don't compromise principles for profit

Strategic Timing

- Consolidate when profitable
- Expand when necessary
- Stay patient with growth

Implementation Guide
Assessment Phase

- Evaluate current operations
- Identify growth opportunities
- Map potential challenges

Planning Phase

- Set clear scaling objectives
- Define quality standards
- Establish communication protocols

Execution Phase

- Implement gradually
- Monitor progress
- Adjust based on feedback

Key Takeaway

Successful scaling isn't just about getting bigger – it's about getting better. It's about building systems that can grow while maintaining quality, staying true to your values while adapting to change, and knowing when to push forward versus when to consolidate gains.

Reflection Questions

1. What aspects of your work could benefit from delegation?
2. How can you better maintain quality as you grow?
3. Are your growth decisions reactive or strategic?

"Remember: The goal isn't just to scale up – it's to scale smart, ensuring that growth strengthens rather than dilutes your vision."

We scale walls to see further, but we build bridges to help others cross.

Ten

Leaving a legacy

Legacy isn't just about what you leave behind – it's about the lives you touch along the way. True impact goes beyond personal achievement; it's about creating ripples of positive change that continue long after you're gone.

Faith as Foundation

Understanding that there's something greater than yourself changes everything about how you approach your purpose. I've learned that having multiple talents isn't just about personal success – it's about responsibility. When you recognize these gifts as blessings from God, especially knowing that many people wish they had talents they could profit from, it shapes how you use them.

This perspective keeps me grounded and grateful. Every achievement becomes an opportunity to give glory to God, acknowledging the source of these abilities. It's about understanding that success isn't just for personal gain – it's a platform for spreading love and light in a world that often feels dark.

Beyond Achievement

The Bible commands us to love others as we love ourselves. This simple but profound directive shapes everything about building a legacy. It's not just about what you accomplish; it's about how you treat people along the way. Making the world better isn't just a noble goal – it's a spiritual calling.

Success without purpose is just achievement. Real legacy comes from:

- Spreading love in practical ways
- Using your platform for positive impact
- Lifting others as you climb

The Development Chain

Just as others helped develop me, I believe in helping develop others. This cycle of growth and giving back creates a continuous chain of positive impact. It's about more than just teaching skills – it's about helping people believe in themselves and in those around them.

The power of belief can transform:

- Individual potential into reality
- Doubt into determination
- Fear into courage

Multi-Generational Impact

True legacy doesn't have age boundaries. I aim to impact everyone:

- Those older than me, showing it's never too late to grow
- My peers, encouraging them to reach higher
- The younger generation, showing them what's possible

Values That Last

The most important values to pass on aren't just about success – they're about character:

- Patience: Understanding that meaningful change takes time
- Love: Making decisions with compassion
- Kindness: Treating others with genuine care
- Peace: Creating harmony in your sphere of influence
- Happiness: Finding and sharing joy in the journey

Creating Ripple Effects

Every person you encounter is fighting battles you might never know about. Your legacy is built in how you respond to these hidden struggles:

- Being the difference someone needs
- Offering help without expecting return
- Creating safe spaces for growth and healing

Practical Legacy
Building Daily Impact

- Look for opportunities to help others
- Share knowledge freely
- Be the positive change you want to see

Relationship Investment

- Build genuine connections
- Mentor where possible
- Support others' dreams

Value Demonstration

- Live your beliefs daily
- Show consistency in actions
- Lead by example

Implementation Guide
Start Where You Are

- Use current influence wisely
- Begin with small acts of kindness
- Build momentum through consistency

Expand Your Impact

- Look for new ways to serve

- Create opportunities for others
- Build systems that empower growth

Sustain Your Influence

- Document lessons learned
- Share wisdom gained
- Create lasting positive change

Key Legacy Principles
Faith-Centered Purpose

- Acknowledge your blessings
- Give glory where due
- Use gifts responsibly

Love-Driven Action

- Make decisions with compassion
- Spread positivity intentionally
- Create inclusive environments

Continuous Development

- Keep growing personally
- Help others grow
- Build lasting impact

Key Takeaway

Your legacy isn't just about what you achieve – it's about who you help, what you give, and how you make others feel. Every day is an opportunity to create positive change that outlasts you.

Final Reflection Questions

1. How are you using your talents to benefit others?
2. What values do you demonstrate daily?
3. How can you create more positive impact in your sphere of influence?

"**Remember: The greatest legacy isn't built in grand gestures, but in daily acts of love, kindness, and service that create lasting positive change in the lives of others.**"

The grind hits different when God guides it. Your hustle becomes holy, your moves become ministry, and your success becomes service. This is just the beginning of what He'll do through you - your legacy is His promise in motion. Keep building with belief, keep moving with meaning, and remember: when faith fuels your future and God holds your blueprint, the only way forward is to hustle with purpose.

Darien Adair is more than just a dreamer—he's a doer. Born and raised in Indianapolis, Indiana, Darien grew up as the youngest of eight siblings, learning early that success isn't handed to you—you have to hustle for it. As a manufacturing manager by day and an entrepreneur by passion, Darien juggles a thriving career with running two clothing brands: one focused on streetwear and the other on luxury fashion.

Through his life experiences, Darien developed a deep love for self-improvement, creative expression, and faith. He believes in grinding with intention and living with purpose, values that inspired the creation of his debut book, Hustle with Purpose. This book reflects his journey—the struggles, lessons, and victories that have shaped him into the man he is today.

Darien's ultimate goal is to leave a legacy—not just for himself, but for others chasing their dreams. When he's not working, designing clothes, or writing, you'll find him having deep conversations, exploring new ideas, and spending time with his wife, Kandace Adair.

You can connect with Darien on social media to follow his journey and learn more about living a purposeful life.

Facebook -@DarienAdair , Instagram -@PilotFlyGuy

DARIEN ADAIR

Closing Statement

As we reach the end of this journey together, I'm reminded of something my brother Mikey used to say: "Ain't nobody colder than you." At first, I thought he was just being supportive. Now I understand he was teaching me something deeper – he saw purpose in my hustle before I did.

This book isn't meant to sit on your shelf as just another success story. It's a call to action. A reminder that you already have everything you need to make your mark on the world. Your talents, your struggles, your faith – they're all part of your unique purpose.

The world doesn't need another person just grinding away. It needs you – with all your gifts, your vision, and your purpose. So take these pages not as a blueprint, but as a spark. Let them ignite whatever fire God has placed in your heart.

> **"First have a purpose, then hustle toward it."** -Darien M Adair

Index

INDEX

A
- Adaptability, 7–13
- in business, 9
- in family life, 7–8
- principles of, 12
- Allen, Alandrius (AD), 8, 33

B
- Balance, 44–50
- work-life, 45
- strategies for, 47
- Bernard, Drew, 21
- Brotherhood, 8–9, 32–33

C
- Communication, 59–60
- in scaling, 59
- with team, 60

D
- Digital distractions, managing, 52
- Doubt, overcoming, 39

E
- Eisenhower Matrix, 53
- Extended family, 33

F
- Faith, 20, 65

- in business, 21
- in decision-making, 27
- Failure, 20-25
- as learning, 20-25
- in business, 22
- Focus, 51-57
- strategies, 54
- maintaining, 55

G
- Goals, 15-16
- setting, 15
- tracking, 16
- Growth, sustainable, 60

H
- Hand-me-downs, lessons from, 8
- Hustle, smart approach to, 14-19

I
- Indianapolis (Naptown), 7

L
- Legacy, 65-70
- building, 67
- principles, 69
- Leadership, 59

M
- Mental strength, 38-43
- building, 40
- exercises, 41
- Mentorship, 33, 68

P
- Patience, 39

- Pivot, 26–31
- knowing when to, 26–28
- strategies for, 28

Q
- Quality control, 61

R
- Resilience, 38–43
- Rest, importance of, 46

S
- Scaling, 58–64
- business, 58–64
- strategies, 61
- Self-doubt, managing, 28, 40, 41
- Support systems, 32–37
- building, 34
- maintaining, 35

T
- Team building, 60
- Time management, 15, 53

V
- Values, 62, 69
- maintaining while scaling, 62
- passing on, 69
- Vision, maintaining, 59

W
- Work-life balance, 45–47

www.ingramcontent.com/pod-product-compliance
Lightning Source LLC
LaVergne TN
LVHW092057060526
838201LV00047B/1438